SELF-ESTEEM:

A TINY BOOK

OF IDEAS

SELF-ESTEEM

What
might
Self-Esteem
refer to?

SELF-ESTEEM

Could we say,
that
Self-Esteem
is HOW we
ESTEEM
OURSELVES:
How we
EVALUATE
Ourselves:
with certain
CRITERIA in mind?

SELF-ESTEEM

SELF-ESTEEM

Now, First,
It looks likely, that we
wish to
Feel GOOD,
about the ASSETS we
have;
But, MOREOVER,
to feel GOOD,
about ALL Aspects
of ourselves...

SELF-ESTEEM

In other words,
to feel "OK" about
any aspects of
ourselves which some
people
find "discomforting"
about us, and may
even
reject us for having,
or seeming to have...

SELF-ESTEEM

Or put it this way,
that we don't end up
REJECTING
OURSELVES,
first and foremost:
in the sense of
SEEING a key TRUTH:
that WHATEVER we
ARE, is as it CAN
ONLY
POSSIBLY BE,
given what what we
were "handed".

SELF-ESTEEM

Hence the phrase,
often heard,
yet not to be dismissed
as trivial:
that "We DID and DO
DO, the BEST we
COULD or CAN,
all things considered.

SELF-ESTEEM

Noting,
of course,
that who we are,
tomorrow, will not be
the
same as we are today,
due to the Law of
Cause and Effect - or
Feedback, one might
say...

SELF-ESTEEM

To put it yet another
way,
that our LIVES,
in each and every
detail,
are utterly
IN ALIGNMENT with
The Laws of the
Universe.

SELF-ESTEEM

Now,
Some people may refer
to this as being
"PERFECT";
or having Self-Love;
Self-Acceptance;
Feeling OK; or
Feeling OK in one's
Skin...

SELF-ESTEEM

SELF-ESTEEM

NEXT...
Or SECONDLY,
or
PART TWO
of Self-Esteem...

SELF-ESTEEM

We surely
CRAVE a SENSE of
USEFULNESS, when
it comes to
to some other PEOPLE.

SELF-ESTEEM

In other words,
we surely want to feel
USEFUL to some other
people, so that we can
"GET" certain "things"
in a Transactional
sense:
Things which we value
and find hard to create
on our own, or to
create
in as efficient a way:

SELF-ESTEEM

Things" such as:
Money;
Sexual experiences;
Being able to be a
SOOTHER of FEARS;
or to help some people
ACCEPT certain things
about themselves;
The support of allies;
"Data";
Validation; or being an
EXAMPLE of
COURAGE.

SELF-ESTEEM

By the way, IF we can
feel no shame over
every aspect of
ourselves, isn't this
something we are
giving to others, as
something highly
useful?
The capacity to help
someone accept
themselves better?

SELF-ESTEEM

One might refer to
these as External
Power
Sources...
Or,
External Assets

SELF-ESTEEM

As contrasted with
what was first
mentioned:
A belief that we are
"OK", that we are
"PERFECT":
Perfectly in alignment,
that is, in Complete
Alignment with
The Laws of the
Universe.
We could refer to this
as Internal Power".

SELF-ESTEEM

So,
to discuss,
or revisit,
the idea of
INTERNAL powers...

SELF-ESTEEM

What more could we
say we most crave,
Internally,
than a sense of
having no SHAME
over any aspect OF
ourselves?
Secondly, to have
no GUILT?
No belief that we have
violated our MORAL
CODE.

SELF-ESTEEM

This set of "self-shamings" including, How our BODIES look; our INTELLIGENCE level, in a rough sense of the word; and how SAVVY we are, about People, and Life in general - whereby we do not want to deem ourselves to be "naive" or a Denier of Reality; or a "fool", thus;

SELF-ESTEEM

Or concerning being
called "lazy"; and how
we "take care" of our
health, and how
proactive we are,
regarding our future,
in general.

SELF-ESTEEM

Even,
acceptance of
the painful effects
that our Existence
has had, of a sort,
to some others,
regardless of how we
are framing this:
saying, perhaps, that
they are or aren't
"taking responsibility
for their own feelings"...

SELF-ESTEEM

Finally, but not least,
HOW we regard
any and all bodily
pains we feel, and
any limitations we
have,
especially, physical
ones...
Or too, how long we
live, before the close of
our life, as we know it.

SELF-ESTEEM

For, might we
consider, that
pain of a physical
or emotional nature
is one thing, but it
likely is magnified
perhaps five times over,
by the SHAME-"pain"
we can often feel,
over the underlying
physical or emotional
suffering?

SELF-ESTEEM

Hence the phrase - the murky advice - "Don't beat yourself up about it"...

SELF-ESTEEM

SELF-ESTEEM

So, to RECAP:
perhaps
We could look at self-esteem - "high self-esteem", or "healthy" self-esteem, or "optimal" self-esteem, as a combination of having value to ourselves, and having value to others...

SELF-ESTEEM

SELF-ESTEEM

We might again
ponder, too, the
POSITIVE impact
we surely have,
when others see OUR
Self-Acceptance,
despite having so-called
"Imperfections".

SELF-ESTEEM

Whereby some others
say, "This person
'accepts' themselves
fully" - "is feeling no
shame over any
aspects of themselves"
-"so maybe I can
somehow adopt this as
my way of living, too,
and stop feeling shame
over aspects of my own
life"...

SELF-ESTEEM

SELF-ESTEEM

By Loran Joly
Copyright 2024

All images
by the
author

email:
message@goldpogo.com